The Next Great Depression

Randall Valentine, PhD.

About the Author

Dr. Randall Valentine is an Assistant Professor of Finance at Georgia Southwestern State University. He has published over 30 articles in Finance and Business Journals. He has also served as a consultant to over 10 national and international corporations. He has been honored by the International Business Society with a distinguished research award.

Table of Contents

Introduction—The Perfect Storm

Chapter 1—The Great Depression

Chapter 2—Credit Scoring

Chapter 3— Financial Modernization Act of 1999

Chapter 4— Role of the Federal Reserve

Chapter 5—9/11, Interest Rates, and the Real Estate Boom

Chapter 6—The Failure of Government

Chapter 7—The Weak Dollar Policy and Inflation

Chapter 8—The Coming Storm

Introduction – The Perfect Storm

When Hurricane Katrina struck the Mississippi and Louisiana Gulf Coast in 2005 with a rage that had not been seen in decades, it was a reminder of how many factors can contribute to the strength of a hurricane. Factors such as water temperature, location of the jet stream, time of high tide, and atmospheric pressure all contribute to the strength of such a storm. In all, there are 13 major factors that influence the strength of a hurricane. For Hurricane Katrina, all 13 were in place to make the storm a major catastrophe. Often, when you hear the environmentalists comment on the storm, they point to global warming and, in particular, the warming of the ocean. Although the earth being warmer certainly may have contributed to the storm being as large and destructive as it was, it was by no means the only factor.

Much like Hurricane Katrina, Democrats often center their blame for the economic downfall on George Bush. And, like in Katrina, he is a contributing factor but he is certainly not the only one. This book is intended to debunk myths, explain the exact causes of this crisis, and forecast what is still to come. As this book will cover, this economic crisis is a result of an intricate and complex web of world events, government legislation, and a failure of banks to regulate themselves. Such factors have led to a worldwide economic depression.

When compared to the great depression, the current crisis in the United States sounds eerily similar. From the factors that led to this point to the responses of government, the parallels are noticeable to the point that the most frequent question I am asked is "Are we in another great depression?" Unfortunately, I am afraid the answer to this question is that we are. This is not to say that another great depression cannot be avoided, it's just that I lack faith in our government to make things better and not worse.

Chapter 1
The Great Depression

The Roaring 1920's

In order to understand the context of The Great Depression, one must look at the 1920's (the Roaring 20's), the period of time that preceded the great depression. The Roaring 20's had a sense of euphoria after WWI along with a sense of optimism that good times were here to stay. In order to aid the transition from a wartime economy to a peacetime economy, the Federal Reserve made the money supply plentiful and kept interest rates low for most of the decade. In addition, the Coolidge administration lowered taxes for all Americans. The result was an economic boom unlike anything the nation had ever seen.

Because the Federal Reserve kept the money supply so loose, individuals could, for the first time, borrow money to invest in the stock market. This allowed individuals of ordinary means to make a great deal of money in stock market speculation. Banks were all too quick to lend money to stock market investors, as the market was increasing exponentially. The result was a booming stock market due to all the individuals who bought stocks. This created a "bubble," making stocks overpriced relative to their earnings. However, since the amount of money being made was in excess of anything the nation had ever seen, banks and stock brokers often encouraged their clients to invest using borrowed money.

With wealth being created at a record pace, homebuilders were erecting homes in mass quantities. For the first time, individuals were buying automobiles. Roads and bridges were being built in mass to accommodate all the cars. In short, the first eight years of the 1920's represented a great time for our nation and economy. However, there were storm clouds on the horizon.

There are many similarities between the Roaring 20's and the late 1990's and early 2000's that will be covered later in this book. The common thread is the extremely loose money supply which provided the fuel needed to create an economic bubble. The Federal Reserve cannot have a longstanding loose fiscal policy without having consequent negative externalities. Specifically, loose fiscal policy creates bubbles, both in the stock market and the real estate market.

The Bubble Bursts
Unfortunately, having a loose monetary policy for an extended period of time doesn't come without collateral damage. When money is plentiful, it causes inflation and the purchasing power of a dollar decreases. The more the treasury prints money, the more money becomes devalued. Further contributing to the inflation problem was the increase in energy prices, which in turn led to an increase in the cost of all goods. With inflation becoming a potential problem to the economy, the Federal Reserve began to raise interest rates in 1928. While the Federal Reserve does not control interest rates, it is important to keep in mind that

it does influence them. When the Federal Reserve wants interest rates to increase, it simply decreases the money supply.

When the Federal Reserve decreased the money supply in the late 1920's, it had a great effect on investors buying stocks with borrowed money. When investors could not borrow to buy stocks, they purchased less. In 1929, the stock market started showing signs of a decline. Although levels held steady, it was clear that the market would not be able to continue its momentum without the plentiful money supply. Soon, rumors of a bubble began to permeate Wall Street and then Main Street. Driven by overpriced stocks and fearful selling, the stock market went down 25% in just 2 days in October of that year. It would not regain its previous levels until 1954, nearly three decades later.

An important distinction exists between the Great Depression and the stock market crash of 1929. Many history books denote that the stock market crash was the start of the great depression. Many academics, including me, postulate that the crash and the great depression were two mutually exclusive events. In our current economic crisis, the stock market and the bank failures happened simultaneously. In the Great Depression, the stock market crashed in 1929 but bank failures did not occur until 1933. It was what happened, or more specifically what did not happen during that period, that caused the bank failures of 1933.

Government Response to the Stock Market Crash
Andrew Mellon, the Treasury Secretary, urged President Herbert Hoover not to overreact to the stock market crash. His belief was that it was a normal market correction and would work itself out over time. However, the newly elected President felt that inaction could be construed as a sign of weakness. He believed that he could fix the problem and gain the confidence of a nation. His belief

was that this would be his capstone in his war on poverty. The problem was that when American wealth seemingly evaporated overnight, there was mounting political pressure for the government to intervene and do something. The problem then was very similar to the problem now in Washington--the pendulum swings to one extreme or the other. The fiscal policy in the 1920's was way too loose. So, the reaction was to tighten the money supply to an opposite extreme. Whether or not Mellon was correct is something we will never know. What followed were the worst economic policies in the history of our government, at least until the last few years.

The first reaction was the passage of the Smoot-Hawley Tariff Act of 1930. This policy put huge tariffs on everything imported into the U.S. and essentially shut down trade with Europe, forcing many European countries to stop paying on loans from WWI. The logic behind the passage of Smoot-Hawley was that the middle class was being hurt by jobs being moved overseas. Hoover thought the passage of this act would enable factories to continue operations in the U.S. What actually happened was the immobilization of worldwide trade, which plunged both Europe and South America into a depression as well. What Hoover failed to realize is that constriction of trade results in the constriction of an economy. If the U.S. is not efficient at producing something, then it shouldn't produce it. Instead of focusing on our distinctive competencies, government focused on trying to support failing industries with catastrophic consequences. Consumer confidence eroded and prices began to deflate due to a lack of demand and a soft job market.

Economists were scrambling to find an answer that would deliver the country out of this severe economic downturn. Soon, the Keynesian economists took over with the theory that an increase in government spending could get us out of any economic downturn. Since tax revenues declined, even with the new tariffs, Hoover felt it was necessary to raise taxes so the government could spend enough to stimulate the economy. In 1932, the U.S. Congress passed one of the largest tax hikes in history. The tax rate on the very wealthy was raised from 25% to 76%. In addition, there was a tax of 15% levied on corporations for the first time. The logic behind the tax increase was tax the wealthy and let the government spend in order to jump start the economy. Since the prevailing view of Washington was that the economic and tax policies of the 1920's had unfairly benefited the rich, taxing the rich in order to facilitate the government stimulated economy seemed the equitable thing to do. The result was an economic catastrophe that actually was the true cause of the Great Depression.

In 1933, Franklin D. Roosevelt took over the Presidency and almost immediately faced a severe crisis. As consumer confidence in banks began to erode, many depositors began to withdraw deposits for fear of bank failures. As rumors of bank failures grew, more and more depositors withdrew money, precipitating the rapid failure of many banks. When this happened, the Federal Reserve curiously left the money supply alone and did not insure any deposits. This inaction left the American public with no confidence in any area of our financial system. Roosevelt responded to this crisis with many acts commonly referred to as the New Deal, which involved mass government spending and government debt. It was not until the start of WWII that the economy was out of a depression.

The New Deal
In the midst of the Great Depression, FDR found himself caught between an economy in shambles and a desire to reform the government into something that matched his political ideals. With unemployment at 25%, credit markets frozen, and foreclosures on the rise, FDR

felt that a series of government initiatives would be the solution to the economy.

The first of the New Deal initiatives was the National Recovery Administration (NRA) which mandated higher minimum wages and restricted work hours and child labor. The problem with this initiative was that it came at a time when businesses were already on the brink of insolvency and could not afford to pay a higher wage. Some economists estimate that the NRA lowered productivity by as much as 40% while goods produced fell by 5%. The NRA was very controversial, to the point where the Supreme Court deemed it unconstitutional.

The interesting thing about the Great Depression is the order in which the dominos fell. The first domino was the stock market, which crashed on consecutive days in 1929. The Hoover initiatives, including tariffs and tax hikes, did little if anything to stimulate the economy. In 1929, government spending did temporarily create more jobs; however, after FDR was elected and the size and scope of government grew, so did unemployment. The more New Deal initiatives were enacted, the more individuals became unemployed. In 1933, banks began to collapse. This was despite the promise of government coming to the rescue of the economy.

During the implementation of the New Deal, advisors within the FDR administration faced the task of trying to balance the budget along with the massive expansion of government spending. However, FDR held steadfast in his belief that the Great Depression was a result of corporate greed and excess competition, which drove wages downward. This in turn led to lower demand and employment. The head of the NRA, Donald Richberg said:
 "There is no choice presented to American business between intelligently planned and uncontrolled industrial operations and a return to the gold-plated

anarchy that masqueraded as "rugged individualism."...Unless industry is sufficiently socialized by its private owners and managers so that great essential industries are operated under public obligation appropriate to the public interest in them, the advance of political control over private industry is inevitable."

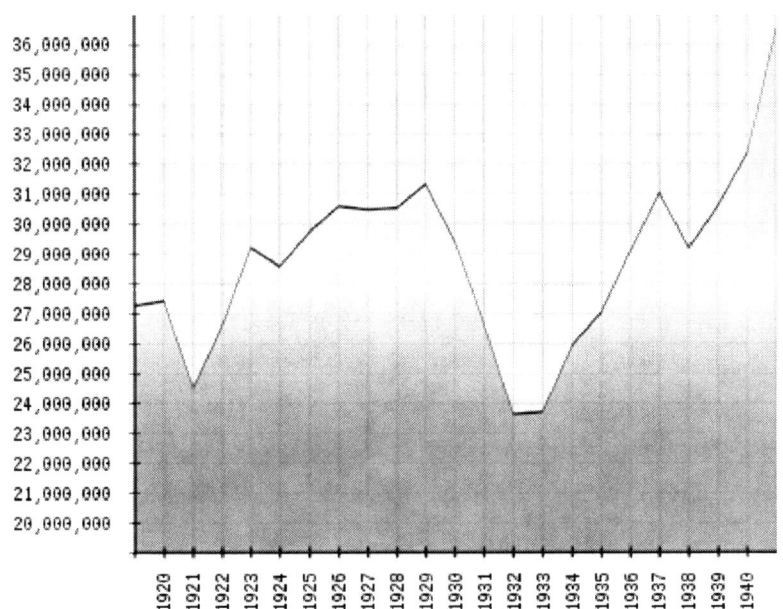

The essence of the lessons learned during the Great Depression is this: Government control and socialized industries do not equate to lower unemployment or a stable economy. To the contrary, both Hoover and FDR proved that excessive government intervention in commerce neither stimulates the economy nor curtails unemployment.

Lessons Learned
There were several effective and important pieces of legislation that came out of the Great Depression. The best piece of legislation coming out of the depression was the Glass-Stegall Act of 1933. This did two important things. First, it created the FDIC and insured all deposits in U.S. banks up to $2,500. This gave depositors confidence that if their bank failed the government would make sure that their money was not lost. The act also allowed the FDIC to have regulatory power over banks, to ensure that balance sheets and lending practices

conformed to a common set of regulatory standards. Second, the act separated investment banking, commercial banking, and insurance. As a result, commercial banks could only accept deposits and make loans such as mortgages. Investment banks could buy, sell, and trade stocks and bonds. Insurance companies were specifically prohibited from doing any bank-like activities. This act made certain that financial institutions would not all fail at the same time. It also gave the public an assurance that each of the three had both the distinctive competencies in their respective fields and the adequate legislation to ensure that there would be no more large scale failures. This act did prevent large scale failure of financial institutions until Gramm-Leach-Bliley repealed the act in 1999.

The other lesson learned from the Great Depression is that protectionism, specifically with tariffs, simply does not work. When the U.S. slaps a tariff on another country, the other nation responds in kind with a tariff of U.S. exports. This means that instead of manufacturing and exporting what we are best at, we are forced to manufacture goods that would be more efficiently produced overseas. In the end, the U.S. consumer pays more for an inferior good rather than being able to shop for a fair market price.

Chapter 2
Credit Scoring

When often asked what the main cause of the current financial crisis is, most people expect me to blame the government or Wall Street. While this crisis is indeed a perfect storm, a convergence of many factors coming together at once, there is one clear factor that can be pointed to. The lending business is often very difficult to fully put your arms around. There is an old saying that "banks will only lend you money when you don't need it." Perhaps in another age of banking, this would hold true. In the information age, computers and statistical programs often determine if, how, and how much you pay for credit. However, these programs weren't developed because of an advance of technology, but as a result of lawsuits brought about by a group of Asians claiming racial discrimination when applying for a mortgage loan.

At virtually every juncture in an individual's life, there is a point in time in which they have to make a major financial decision. Should I buy this house? Should

I buy this car? Which credit card offer should I accept? How should I pay off my debt? Which debt should I pay off first? Where should I go for a loan?

The answers to these questions can be quite perplexing. However, understanding an individual's credit is even more perplexing. The premise of credit scoring is that it is supposed to give an accurate representation to lenders whether or not an individual will repay the loan as agreed. This is a color, gender, and age blind system. That, however, is the only good thing I can say with regard to credit scoring. The true premise behind credit scoring is to con and explicitly rip off the consumer, deluding you into believing that you should pay a higher interest rate or accept unfair loan terms.

The credit reporting companies understand that knowledge is power. That is why they keep the system as complicated as can be. Solving the puzzle of what exactly will affect which of your 3 credit scores can be as perplexing as solving the mystery of the JFK assassination. The system is unbelievably complex yet has a clear and decisive purpose, to keep your power at bay.

The Most Important Number in Your Life
The enigma of a credit score is the most important number in your financial existence. For every 20 or so points that your credit score decreases, it costs you money and lots of it. The following is a chart gathered from our friends at Fair Isaac, a credit reporting company commonly referred to as FICO.

As you improve your FICO® scores, you pay less when you buy on credit - whether purchasing a home loan, cell phone, a car loan, or signing up for credit cards. For example, on a $150,000 30-year, fixed-rate mortgage:

Your FICO® Score	Your interest rate	Your monthly payment
760 - 850	5.48%	$850
700 - 759	5.7%	$871
680 - 699	5.88%	$887
660 - 679	6.09%	$908
640 - 659	6.52%	$950
620 - 639	7.07%	$1,005

As you can see, your payment can dramatically increase or decrease based on your credit score. If your credit score falls only by a few points, then you could potentially pay thousands more every year in interest and other fees. Thus, the importance of this credit score is enormous. Points on your credit score equate to money. For every point your score is higher, you receive a lower interest payment. For every point your score is lower, you receive a higher interest payment. It is that plain and simple. The primary objective of this book is to explain the logic and methodology (or lack thereof) behind how an individual's credit score is computed.

The 500 Billion Dollar Industry of Raising Your Credit Score

For years I have used an e-mail account at Yahoo! mail. Every time I check my mail various advertisements will appear on the screen. Two of the most frequent ads offer to check your credit score for free and claim that they can raise your credit score. This is not big business, this is HUGE business. Websites like myfico.com advertise to help you raise your credit score for a fee. The three credit reporting agencies (Trans Union, Equifax, and Experian) commonly charge $12.95 or higher to provide your credit report and score. The more you inquire about your score, the more you will pay. There are also monthly credit monitoring services that will provide a regular update of your report and score for a monthly fee.

The sad thing is that in some ways this is a very necessary purchase. For reasons to be explained in chapter 4, regularly checking both your credit report and credit score is very much a necessity. This 500 billion dollar business exists because financial professionals, much less consumers, do not understand credit scoring. Because THEY keep you guessing, you must pay to find out the answers. The game of credit scoring has become a game of high stakes, with the consumer making nothing more than an educated guess at what might optimize their credit score.

If a detective looks at who committed a crime, the first thing they look at is motive. Who did it and why did they do it? For an individual to commit a crime, they must have a motive. Was it greed, jealousy, lust, anger, or insanity? To understand why the credit scoring system is so flawed, you must look at why it was created, who perpetuated it, and most importantly who has the motive or who profits from this system. The above mentioned institutions are the ones who profit from this system.

Banks, Insurers, Mortgage Lenders, and Auto Finance Companies

The purpose of credit scoring is that it is supposed to predict how likely you are to repay a loan. The higher your credit score, the more likely will make loan or credit card payments. The lower your score, the more you have to pay. So if you pay more interest, these entities benefit and their profits increase. That reason alone is the bottom line for credit scoring. Using the above table, you see that the lower your credit score is, the more interest you will pay. If you purchase a house, this means that you cannot spend as much on a house as you would otherwise be able to. It, in no way, benefits you to pay more for interest. So if your credit score is low, you must be a bad credit risk, right? Not so, but this book will address that a little later.

For the most part, banks and mortgage lenders do not hold the loan that make for you. They simply originate the loan and sell it to a third party. The higher the interest rate, the more they can sell your loan for. I cannot tell you how many clients have told me that they did not think they were getting a good interest rate, and in most cases they were correct. However, since real estate contracts are finite, they didn't have the time to go to another lender and start the process all over without risking losing the property. Unfortunately, consumers only have leverage when they re-finance, when they are able to switch from one lender to another. However, as I will explain later, this also has limitations. When concerned customers come to me seeking advice, I usually tell them that if they want the property then they simply have to bite the bullet and take the higher rate of interest.

The New Big 3
In the past, GM, Ford, and Chrysler were considered "the big 3." Since their demise,

the new big 3 are Experian, Equifax, and Transunion. These companies are the gatekeepers in the financial world. They collect credit information about you. Based on this information, they calculate their own version of the all too important credit score. The problem is that the information they report is easily inaccurate and the score they calculate is downright inaccurate.

Anybody Can Report You for Anything......Really
Anytime someone seeks my advice about a major purchase they intend to finance, I always advise that they obtain a copy of their credit report first. At least half the time, there is always a surprise waiting on them. I had one friend who found out that he owed child support in a state he had never been to. Others have credit cards on their report that are not theirs. Many others find out they have late payments for erroneous reasons. The most common error, however, is they find some bogus collection item on their report.

I regularly pull a copy of my credit report (which I have to pay for) simply to ensure the accuracy of what's on it. Perhaps the most outrageous item ever to appear on my report was a collection item from HealthSouth, a company whose demise came as the result of accounting fraud. The accusation was that they billed me for $64 and I paid $56 and stiffed them on the other $8. Logically is makes no sense that they would bill me for $64 and I would send in a check for only $56. Nonetheless, they placed my account into collections for $8 without my knowledge. Having a single item in collections can drop your credit score by as much as 100 points, which can prevent you from getting a loan. But, the logical question is: If someone does not pay a bill for $8, does that make them a credit risk?

The underlying problem with credit reports is that there are little to no standards for reporting a collection. You are given 30 days to respond to an accusation of a debt. If you don't respond, then it could end up on your credit report. I always urge any client or student to respond to any accusation of a debt if they feel it is in any way not valid. It is the only way to prevent some arbitrary debt from ending up on your credit report.

What is a Credit Score
Every semester, I always ask my class a simple question: If you were a banker, what is the most important factor you would look at when evaluating an individual's credit application? The most common answer is always "have they paid their bills on time in the past?" The second most frequent answer is "do they have money and income to pay their bills in the future?" I then ask what percentage of your credit score is made up of these 2 factors. I always hear 50%, 70%, and even 100%. When I tell them that the real answer is that payment history is only 30% and your income doesn't count at all, the students are often stunned. They don't understand why this

is. When you look at some of the weird things about credit scoring there are some things that stand out.

----Your past payment history, specifically paying your bills on time, only accounts for 30% of your credit score.
----Points are deducted from your credit score every time your credit is checked. Every time you get insurance, utilities, try to shop around for a mortgage or auto loan, or apply for any new credit your score is lowered. As a result, consumers are prohibited from shopping around for the best deals.
----If you close an account, points are deducted from your score. So, if you pay a mortgage or a car loan you would think you would be rewarded. The opposite is true. If you pay off an account and that account is closed, you are penalized. So, in the world of credit scoring, pay your bills on time but don't EVER pay anything off.
----Anytime you open a new account, points are deducted from your score. If

you re-finance a mortgage to receive a lower payment, you are given a double deduction for opening a new account and closing an old one. Then if your mortgage is sold to another lender, you will have points deducted even though you did nothing at all.

----Credit scores are maximized when you have exactly two major credit cards. If you have no credit cards, which most financial advisors would say is a good thing, your score is penalized.

----If you have credit cards and carry no balances on them, you are penalized. You must carry between 35% and 70% balances on your TWO cards in order to maximize your score. This is truly counterintuitive to all logic.

----The types of loans you have greatly affect your credit score. For instance, having multiple mortgages for rental property will lower your score.

How Did Credit Scoring Contribute to the Financial Crisis?

There are major flaws in our tax accounting system. We have a progressive tax system, where theoretically the rich pay a higher percentage of their income in taxes than the poor do. However, this really doesn't work. Warren Buffet has a famous saying, "my secretary pays more taxes than I do." The object for tax accountants is to use as many deductions as possible, such as cars, meals, and depreciation, to minimize taxable income. Thus, a small business, although cash rich, may report very little in the way of income to the IRS. Since small business owners have no W2's, their tax returns represent their only form of income. Since this income is purposefully low, mortgage lenders came up with a "stated" income system. If individuals had a good enough credit score, they could get a 100% loan on a mortgage simply by stating to the lender what their real income was.

Prior to an age of credit scoring, bankers used a "sniff test" to discern if individuals were actually making enough money to pay back a loan. For instance, if the applicant owns a restaurant you go to and the establishment always is packed, then it could be determined that the low income was a product of creative accounting and not a factual reality. The problem is that when banks started using the credit scoring system, if some individual came in with the same credit score and was denied a loan, they could enact a lawsuit on the basis of discrimination. Thus, instead of having an antitrust exemption like insurance companies, banks and mortgage lenders were held to the credit scoring standard. Insurance companies can raise rates or deny coverage on the basis of gender, age, and marital status. If banks did this, they would get sued.

What this amounts to is that a complicated tax code in addition to an equally complex credit scoring system leads to a lack of efficiency in credit markets. Simply put, lenders were forced to make loans they later admitted knew were at a high probability for default. If banks were unable to lend money to small business owners due to a lack of verifiable income, then credit markets and business would freeze.

For instance, Joe Smith, a local building contractor, comes into the bank with an extensive background of re-paying debt on time and a credit score of 720. The loan officer is actually financing three clients for whom Joe is building a house for. So, he clearly has income. However, he also has a very talented and creative CPA who found a way to limit his adjusted gross income to $11,000. Joe claims to have an actual income of at least $150,000, but that amount cannot be verified by a tax return or W2. Joe wants a $250,000 loan to purchase a home. The bank clearly would give Joe the loan.

The very same day, a Brazilian immigrant comes into the bank with a 720 credit score. They claim to be self employed, although there is little verification of this. On their tax return, they have income of $15,000. They have no history with the bank nor do they have an account there. If the bank were to deny the loan, they would subject themselves to potential litigation along with a possible government crackdown for discrimination against immigrants and minorities.

Two years ago, one of my students came into my office to tell me he was having some trouble getting a copy of his credit report. He wanted my help but was ashamed that I would see his credit. He said, "I just know my score is going to be horrible." When I asked him why, he told me that he had two visa cards that were both maxed to the limit and five years of student loans that he had not made his first payment on. When I heard that, I told him that his score was going to be very high. I was correct. His credit score was 780, putting him in the top 3% of credit applicants. This means that during the real estate boom of 2003-2006, this student could have purchased a multi-million dollar home with no money down—even though he was a full-time student who was not gainfully employed. During that time, banks and mortgage companies were making these loans as quickly as they could. As long as housing prices went up, individuals who could not really afford the house they purchased could sell the home and make a profit prior to it being foreclosed on. Banks would make their money back, and individuals were selling their homes for a profit. So, everyone was happy during the years that real estate kept increasing in price.

Chapter 3
Financial Modernization Act of 1999

The year 1999 was an incredibly important one in the financial markets. To understand the context of the moment, we should first examine the context of what happened during the 1990's and the internet boom. The stock market was increasing at a frightening pace. During that time, many banks including Citigroup were complaining about what they perceived to be outdated depression era legislation that prohibited banks from competing on a larger, global scale. Specifically, banks and other financial institutions sought to repeal Glass-Steagall, a 1933 depression era act that separated the activities of commercial banking, investment banking, and insurance. The purpose of the legislation was to explicitly prevent the failure of mega-banks as seen in 1933.

The Glass-Steagall Act of 1933 was largely in response to the failure of commercial banks during the Great Depression. Glass-Steagall created the FDIC, which insures commercial bank deposits. This allows no other entity, such and investment banks and insurers, to accept deposits. The purpose of this act was to ensure that the great depression era "run on the banks" would not repeat itself. This act did prevent the occurrence of such during its duration.

The 1933 "run on the banks" was largely created not only by the failure on banks' balance sheets but also by a failure of government to convince consumers that their money was safe. If a bank went under during that time, the depositor lost their money with no hope of return. Thus, when a bank was even rumored to be going under, depositors would literally line up around the corner to get their money. When banks ran out of money, they were done. There was no government backed insurance to give consumers the benefit of a safety net. In my opinion, this act was the single greatest success of New Deal legislation. So naturally, our government threw it out the window in 1999.

The Financial Modernization Act (FMA) of 1999 (also known as Gramm-Leach-Bliley) repealed the separation of financial entities. The logic behind this act was that it would allow commercial banks to compete on a fair playing field with investment banks. What the act actually did was allow investment banks and insurers to operate as commercial bank-like institutions, offering deposits, checking accounts, and loans. At the urging of major financial institutions like Citigroup, President Clinton signed the Financial Modernization Act into law on November 12th, 1999. What followed was a vast string of mergers and acquisitions among commercial banks, investment banks, and insurers. As a result, you can now go into any commercial bank to trade stocks and buy insurance products. For example, you could have a checking account at Merrill Lynch and trade stocks at Bank of America.

Effects on Investment Banking

In 1999, there were five major investment banking firms: Merrill Lynch, Bear Stearns, Goldman Sachs, Leyman Brothers, and Morgan Stanley. The Gramm-Leach-Bliley Act allowed these companies to vastly expand their product lines to include commercial banking and insurance. Of particular importance was the fact that these institutions were now allowed to invest in mortgages and mortgage backed securities. This allowed for a great expansion for these firms for the first seven years after FMA was enacted. In particular, when real estate boomed in the early 2000s as a result of the very loose money supply, these firms were able to post record profits primarily due to their highly profitable mortgage lending units. However, these newfound powers soon backfired when the traditional investment banks were caught in the midst of the subprime mortgage meltdown.

Prior to 1999, investment banks would not be allowed to invest in mortgages at all. The FMA policy change, along with the loose monetary policy of the Federal Reserve during the ensuing time period, made residential mortgages the most profitable part of the investment banking business. When the real estate market crashed, the investment banks were taken down along with commercial banks, but to an even more extreme. Of the original five major investment banking firms, only Goldman Sachs and Morgan Stanley have survived. Had the FMA Act never been passed, the subprime mortgage collapse never would have happened.

Effects on Insurers
The major domino to fall in the insurance industry was the American Insurance Group (AIG), the largest insurer in the U.S. They are now 80% owned by the federal government as part of a massive $85 billion bailout. They, much like the investment banks, had heavy exposure to the U.S. mortgage markets. Had FMA never been passed, AIG would have never been on the verge of bankruptcy or

required $150 Billion in government bailouts to remain solvent.

Summation of Major Effects
Had the FMA of 1999 never been enacted, it can be argued that commercial banks would have suffered but that investment banks and insurers would have largely gone unscathed. All three major areas of our financial economy, which had been separated, are now in the same sinking boat. The wisdom of such decisions is now highly questioned and the fallout has put our economy in peril.

An argument could be made that had FMA never been passed, we would not be facing the Next Great Depression. First, there would have not been the vast proliferation of mortgage lending in the first place. If major players like Merrill Lynch and AIG had never engaged in the mortgage market, there would not have been such an availability and variety of mortgage products available. Without the expansion of mortgage lending, it is unlikely that we would have even had an explosion in real estate prices that caused a bubble. However, even if FMA had never been passed, the U.S. would have still have had some problems due to the other government regulation that pertained to Fannie Mae and Freddie Mac.

The Expanded Role of Fannie and Freddie
In 1999, President Clinton directed Fannie Mae and Freddie Mac to aggressively make subprime mortgage loans to the poor and especially to minorities. The *New York Times* hailed this action for letting those who had no opportunity to own a home to finally have that privilege.

I have no problem with the government trying to give the less fortunate a hand up in society. However, there is often an inherent problem with this. One of my former colleagues had a unique poster in his office that was a picture of fast food French fries with the caption "Not

Everyone Grows up to be a Rocket Scientist." Likewise, not everyone should get a mortgage. Unfortunately, this is true. Some individuals simply are not financially responsible enough to own a home. The problem Freddie and Fannie had was simple - they HAD to make subprime mortgage loans or answer to the government. Essentially, they were forced by the failed government policy of Bill Clinton and later George Bush to give loans that they knew were going to default. This, in combination with the irresponsible policies of the Federal Reserve, contributed to the crisis being as severe and painful as it is.

Chapter 4
Role of the Federal Reserve

The Federal Reserve (FED) was created in 1913 with several purposes. First, their primary purpose was to add stability to the banking system, positioning themselves as a bank to banks. In doing so, they were charged with the power to regulate banks and the banking system. Second, the Federal Reserve was given control over the nation's money supply. With this power they want to maximize employment, to moderate long-term interest rates, and to stabilize long term prices and thereby moderate inflation.

Over the years, the powers of the Federal Reserve have greatly expanded. With control over the money supply, they have great influence over bank interest rates and the economy in general. Often the media will report that the FED is raising or lowering interest rates. This is an inaccurate claim. The Federal Reserve does not dictate the interest rate at which banks can loan money, but they can influence it. If the FED wishes for interest rates to increase, they can decrease the money supply. When the money supply decreases, this makes money harder to come by for banks to loan out. This contracts economic growth, which is often used by the FED as a prescription for inflation.

There are many dangers of Federal Reserve policy. If interest rates are kept low and the money supply is loose for too long it can contribute to inflation, like the U.S. experienced in the late 1970's. If the FED keeps interest rates high and decreases the money supply, then the economy will fail to grow and often go into recession, like the U.S. experienced in 2000. Thus, the FED tries to moderate growth when the economy is good and to spur growth when the economy is bad. The major problem with FED policy lies not with their identification of the problems of recession or inflation but with their overreaction of policy. After the threat of inflation began to surface in 2005, the FED hiked interest rates 18 times after that. That overreaction is what caused the real estate market to plummet rather than to level off.

There are striking parallels between FED policy preceding The Great Depression and FED policy preceding our current recession. During the 1920's, the FED kept interest rates low and the monetary policy very loose. This no doubt contributed to the robust economic growth during the first part of that decade. During the 1990's, Allan Greenspan, Chair of the FED, also kept interest rates low for the better part of the decade. He did this for a couple of reasons. First, oil prices were at relatively low levels which kept inflation levels moderate. Second, the proliferation of the internet caused the economy and the stock market to grow at a record pace, similar to the Roaring 20's.

In 1928, the FED was concerned that there was a growing problem with inflation. Starting in the early part of that year, they contracted the money supply 14 times, thereby bringing economic activity to a significant slowdown. More importantly, since much of the money used to buy stocks during the 1920's was borrowed money, the stock market suffered. Without money coming into banks and financial institutions, it became difficult to sustain stock market levels. The quickness and severity by which the FED contracted the money supply was a clear catalyst for the rapid October crash of the stock market in 1929.

In the last decade, the FED has rapidly contracted the money supply on two separate occasions. The first time was at the end of the 1990's. With the stock market booming and the tech sector doing very well because of the internet, Greenspan referred to the stock market as "irrational exuberance" during congressional testimony. Clearly, he was inferring that we were in a stock market speculation bubble. Since the FED kept money plentiful, many more individuals were able to participate in the stock market upturn. Adding to the participation levels for the first time was the inception of online stock trading, which enabled individuals to purchase stocks for a low transaction costs.

The FED contracting the money supply had a drastic effect starting in 2000, when the stock market started to take a downturn. The FED cited rising inflationary pressures and long term price stabilization as the rationale for cutting the money supply. They vowed that the "stagflation" period of high inflation and low growth would never again be repeated. The economy soon was beginning a recession. The recession was made worse in 2001 as a result of 9/11.

After 9/11, Greenspan again had a 4-year long policy of historically low interest rates and loose money supply. However, there was a big difference between the late 1990's and 2005. Oil prices were steadily rising during the decade and had doubled from the lows of the previous decade. This created inflationary pressures not seen during the previous decade. Business heavily rely on transportation to move goods from one location to another. For example, every good on a grocery store shelf is trucked, shipped, or flown to its end location. If the price of gas increases, then the price of that good on the store shelf increases also. This is primarily what causes inflation.

Greenspan cited low interest rates and a loose money supply as the main causes of inflation during that period. In order to remedy the inflation problem, Greenspan began a policy of contracting the money supply. After his term as FED Chair expired, he was replaced by Princeton Economics Professor Ben Bernake, who was a scholar of The Great Depression. When Bernake took the office, he pledged to continue Greenspan's policy of fighting inflation and wanted to mold himself into the reputation of being someone who would continue to fight inflation.

Between Greenspan and Bernake, the FED contracted the money supply 18 times. The effects of the rapid decrease of the money supply will be examined in the following chapter.

The FED certainly did do some things right. After 9-11, making the money supply loose for a period was the right thing to do. This gave banks the infusion of cash they needed in order to make loans to consumers and businesses alike. The problem is that often when the FED makes a move they tend to overreach. The FED kept the money supply very loose through 2004, long past when the economy was out of the recession.

When oil prices began to rise and inflation set in, the loose money policy became a bit worrisome for the FED. Instead of incrementally increasing interest rates and waiting for the appropriate economic data to reflect their moves, they recklessly raised interest rates 18 times. Instead of the housing market cooling off, it crashed due to the constriction of cash by the FED.

Chapter 5
9/11, Interest Rates, and the Real Estate Boom

The terrorist attacks of 9/11 left a lasting impression on our nation. Outside of the horrific images being broadcast on television, the one thing I remember about 9/11 was my shopping trip to Wal Mart. Usually, my shopping trips are accompanied by run-ins with friends, co-workers, and even individuals you would rather not see. In short, Wal Mart was a place where you must run into someone you know. It was always busy, even to the point of having trouble of getting your cart up and down the aisle. Truthfully, it was usually a trip I dreaded. When I went to the store that night, it resembled a ghost town. Other than the employees, I was the only person there. It occurred to me at this point that not only businesses in New York, but American businesses everywhere were going to greatly suffer as a result of the attacks. Simply put, individuals were watching television and not shopping. Even that night, it just didn't seem right.

It is important to remember that 9/11 was a direct attack on our financial infrastructure. The stated goal of Al Qaeda was to cripple our economy. Although the attacks of 9/11 did make a recession worse, our economy did recover.

In the aftermath of 9/11, Greenspan rapidly added liquidity to the markets and increased the money supply. In fact, he went all the way to the historical lows of 1% interest rates. This accomplished the FED's goal of stimulating economic growth. However, it did one other thing. It created a boom in the real estate market by having a loose monetary policy. Since money was easy to come by, banks could loan out more that ever before. Also, Fannie Mae and Freddie Mac could now participate in the Sub-Prime mortgage market because of a Presidential order by Bill Clinton in 1999. This allowed for many of the "stated" income mortgages that today have the highest default rates.

Stated income loans traditionally were meant for use by small business owners who underreported their income on tax returns. For example, a restaurant owner may have a high gross income but have a very good accountant who minimizes their taxable income. In addition, there may be cash sales which are not reported at all. A local banker who frequents the restaurant can verify that the business is doing very well. The banker can give a mortgage loan based on "stated" income, meaning that there is no income verification requirement. The problem is that due to credit scoring and discrimination laws, if the local restaurant owner with a 700 credit score is able to get a stated income loan then anyone with a 700 credit score is entitled to the same loan.

As a result of the stated income loans, speculators began buying real estate based on stated income loans. Often, no down payment was required to get these loans. Investors with a sufficient credit score could buy as many of the properties as they wished. Investors would buy properties and often turn or flip them, earning a quick profit.

In some areas of the country, such as Florida and California, real estate price were up as much as 350%. This created the type of speculative bubble that leads to widespread economic downturns. The interesting thing to note is that unlike the "irrational exuberance" speech, neither Greenspan nor Bernake sounded the warning bell that the real estate market was establishing unsustainable prices.

Starting in the latter part of 2005, Greenspan and then Bernake started contracting the money supply in order to stave off inflation. This policy to curb inflation was an abject failure. Not only did they fail to curb inflation, but inflation rapidly increased. From February 2005 to February 2008, food prices alone increased 81%. Ironically, much of Ben Bernake's research has to do with the premise of oil being the primary driver of inflation. He must have forgotten this when he repeatedly raised interest rates to try to stop inflation.

What the FED did not recognize and government officials still fail to acknowledge is that the primary driver of inflation is oil prices and not a loose money supply. The FED could do absolutely nothing to stop inflation. What they did do led to the demise of the real estate market, banks, and the economy as a whole. Many of the mortgages taken out during the real estate boom were adjustable rate mortgages, which have a low introductory interest rate that rises in 1, 3, or 5 years to a higher rate of interest. With the FED contracting the money supply, the individuals with adjustable rate mortgages could not re-finance their mortgages due to the lack of available funds. Also, individuals who sought to buy a home now found it more difficult to get a home loan. This created a snowball effect, where sales decreased and then totally fell off the map. If the FED had not decreased the money supply 18 times from 2005 to 2007, then there would have been a real estate slowdown but there is also a high probability there would have been no crash and no "Great Recession" or worse yet the Next Great Depression.

The underlying problem throughout this real estate crash is that buyers can't get loans and lenders don't have the money to lend. This was a result of the FED's contractionary fiscal policy. By the time the FED recognized that banks were in trouble in 2007 and began to increase the money supply, the damage had already started and proved at this point to be unstoppable. Now, interest rates have been cut to 0%, banks have been given a $700 billion bailout, and credit markets still have yet to move to the point where the real estate market has begun to recover.

As happened when the stock market crashed in 1929, many economists blame the FED for creating a bubble by keeping interest rates too low for too long. Had the money supply never been so high, there would have not been adequate capital for banks and other lending institutions to lend to create a bubble in the first place. Thus, many of the problems that created the real estate downturn can be directly traced to 9/11 and the rise in oil prices. Clearly, the FED overreacted both times, first by keeping interest rates at 1% for nearly 3 years and then by raising rates too far too fast. Ironically, much of Ben Bernake's research points to the FED causing the Great Depression by its monetary policy. Could it be that history has repeated itself?

Chapter 6
The Failure of Government

Perhaps the most frustrating thing about the most recent election season was the finger pointing of politicians. Democrats blamed George Bush for everything and Republicans criticized Wall Street greed and lack of oversight. The one thing at which Washington is truly talented is blaming everyone other than themselves for the horrible state of our economy. The question I am most frequently asked is "who is really to blame?" That answer to that question is very complicated, mainly because there is so much blame to spread.

Government has a way of overcomplicating things. If something works, it is thrown out because of some fear or ideological principle. Take for instance the Glass-Steagall Act of 1933, the legislation that separated commercial banks, investment banks, and insurance companies. The rationale behind the legislation was that banks could not grow to the point that their failure would threaten the economy as a whole. For 66 years, the legislation accomplished its purpose in keeping massive, widespread economic failures to a minimum. This is not to say that there weren't failures in isolated sectors like the savings and loan failure in the 1980's or the stagflation of the 1970's. During the time this legislation was effective, there was no large scale threat of a major financial institution going under and threatening the economy as a whole.

There certainly could have been an argument made that due to the technology revolution and the globalization of financial markets that Glass-Steagall needed to be amended to where institutions could compete on a global level. In the enacting of Gramm-Leach-Bliley, there were several mistakes made. First, Citigroup authored major parts of the legislation. If you ask how this could happen, the answer is simple: Citigroup donated the appropriate amount to the re-election campaigns of some key people in congress. Second, there was a misconception that total deregulation was the only option that would work in order for our financial market prosper. History tells us that pure capitalism totally unregulated will ultimately implode on itself. The other thing history tells us is that over-regulation will constrict economic growth to the point that businesses flee the country. It is important to note that the Gramm-Leach-Bliley act was passed by a 98-2 vote in the Senate. Thus, both parties were to blame.

The Origin of the Fannie and Freddie Problems

I recently came across an article from the New York Times in 1999 that showered praise on the Clinton administration for allowing Freddie and Fannie to give sub-prime mortgage loans to borrowers with low income. This would accomplish the administration's goal of increasing home ownership. The article also heaped praise on Franklin Raines, who at the time was the Fannie Mae CEO and today is a chief economic advisor to Barack Obama.

When George Bush took office, he also urged Fannie and Freddie to maximize home ownership. During his second state of the union address to the nation, Bush bragged that home ownership was an all time high. As we now know, the major problem with this was that people with low income did not benefit by being allowed to purchase a house they could not afford. Fannie and Freddie were the first to fail among all major lending institutions, and they failed to the point of needing a $200 billion federal bailout to stay solvent.

While it is a laudable goal to promote the virtues of home ownership and to try to make loans affordable to everyone, it is clearly not the prudent thing to do. This is not only a failure of government but also of our educational system. In public schools, children are taught to read, write, and do arithmetic. However, almost every student who graduates from an American high school is financially illiterate. They don't understand mortgages, escrow accounts, insurance, or taxes. Most of all, they don't know if they really can afford to take on a mortgage. This is truly unfortunate. While government pushes home ownership, it fails to educate individuals about any of the intricacies of finance.

The Fallout from Accounting Fraud
In 2002, there were several companies that failed. The important part of the story was that massive accounting fraud was used to conceal that the companies fudged the numbers, making profits artificially higher. There was public outrage, specifically for Enron and World Com, whose executives made millions while the employees saw much of their retirement accounts vanish. It was truly heartbreaking to hear the stories of individuals who had lost what they had worked all their lives for.

In response to this, congress held multiple hearings to determine what happened. The irony of the congressional hearings was that many of the congressmen and congresswomen were every bit as dishonest about hiding where their campaign contributions were coming from as the CEO's were about inflating profits. The hearings were the usual dog and pony show, with the Washington elite acting enraged and the CEOs sidestepping every substantive question.

Congress made the decision to act swiftly and harshly, and passed the Sarbanes-Oxley Act of 2002 requiring strict oversight of the accounting procedures of all public corporations. This act went way too far, and U.S. corporations have spent $1.6 trillion in compliance costs--money that could have been used for investing in the infrastructure of the company or to hire employees. Think of it in these terms: Congress just passed a $700 billion bailout to "stimulate" our economy. How much would the U.S. economy have been "stimulated" over the last 6 years if corporations had an additional $1.6 trillion to invest and hire new employees?

As a result of the Sarbanes-Oxley act, thousands of companies de-listed from the NYSE and NASDAQ and left for foreign markets where government regulation is more favorable. Again, pure capitalism left unchecked will ultimately implode on itself. However, regulation which is too strict and goes too far will also cripple the economy. Does the government ever do anything in moderation?

2006---The Start of the Financial Collapse
In 2006, the Iraq war was going badly. Exasperated voters then elected Democrats to Congress, with the promise that they would get us out of Iraq. As we now know, this did not happen. One of the promises made by the new Speaker of the House, Nancy Pelosi, was that this Congress would be the most ethical and transparent Congress in history. At the time, there were cries that the Bush administration lied about the intelligence on Iraq in the first place.

When the Democrats took over Congress, Chris Dodd was appointed as the head of the Senate Banking committee. As head of this committee, his charge is to provide oversight into banking practices, ensuring that banks are run soundly and are making the appropriate dealings. At the time of his appointment in 2006, banks were financially sound. At some point during the last two years, many banks have come to the point of collapse. At no time did Senator Dodd sound an alarm that something was amiss. As a matter of fact, during the beginning stages of the collapse he re-affirmed that the banking system was solid and that excess worry was unfounded.

We now know that the statements Dodd made were either misguided, naïve, or an outright lie. Did he lack the proper acumen or training to discern whether or not banks were indeed heading toward a collapse? If this were the case, then it stands to reason that he would probably never have been appointed to the position in the first place. After banks started to collapse, troubling news was reported about Dodd. First, he received more campaign contributions from Fannie and Freddie than any other politician…ever. Second, he was the beneficiary of a 2% loan from Countrywide, a mortgage lender who was acquired by J.P. Morgan Chase as part of a government brokered bailout. Since market rates at the time of Dodd's loan were 6%, did he look the other way to unsound banking practices as a means of returning a favor to Countrywide? Also, since Fannie and Freddie received $250 billion in federal bailouts, did Dodd betray his fiduciary duties by taking campaign contributions from a company that the taxpayers had to bail out? Whatever the case may be, it doesn't look good for a chairman of the Senate Banking committee to be taking donations and below board mortgage loans from the very institutions to which the taxpayers entrust him to oversee. Neither the Bush administration nor Congress has called for an investigation. Perhaps he should be prosecuted like the fallen corporate executive who misled their shareholders.

Also in 2006, Barney Frank was appointed head of the financial services committee, which is in charge of oversight of all non-bank financial institutions such as insurance companies, investment banks, and Freddie and Fannie. Like Dodd, his oversight can be described as nothing short of an abject failure. In June of 2008, Frank appeared on CNBC affirming his faith that Freddie and Fannie were financially solid. In September, the treasury cut them a $250 billion check to keep them solvent. Did Frank miss something? We know that, like Dodd, he did take some campaign contributions from Freddie and Fannie though it was a much lesser amount. We also know that in June he either was a hopeless optimist or delusional. So who does Frank blame during his 2008 re-election campaign? Of course George Bush is to blame. Again, there is no one in Washington that doesn't play the blame game.

The final player in the meltdown is Chris Cox, a Bush appointee as Chair of the Securities and Exchange Commission (SEC). He is in charge of federal oversight of all securities that are traded, such as stocks and bonds. This includes mortgage backed securities that group mortgages together and sell them as one security. The problem is that the SEC knew this practice was going on and did absolutely nothing to regulate it. Also, Cox failed to sound any warning alarm that a crisis resulting from these securities was going to happen.

I have given much thought to Dodd, Frank, and Cox. If any one of these three individuals had done their job, much of our current financial meltdown could have been either avoided or to some extent negated. Together, these three individuals failed their positions, their country, and the integrity of the American taxpayers. In short, these three form an Axis of Incompetence, the only way in which they can be described.

Finally, the Bush administration takes a huge amount of blame for the failure of government. Every Bush appointee from Cox to Bernake to Treasury Secretary Hank Paulson failed to sound any kind of alarm that there might be a problem. Again, any one of the three could have done something to make this situation turn out much better than it has.

Chapter 7
The Weak Dollar Policy and Inflation

In the early part of the century, the U.S. basically printed very little money. This is primarily attributed to the U.S. being on the gold standard, a system where dollars could be freely exchanged for a pre-determined fixed amount of gold. At the time, most developed countries were on the gold standard. Even though the U.S. possessed much of the world's gold, the amount of money in print remained relatively static until 1933, when FDR officially raised the price of gold, allowing more money to fund the New Deal expenditures.

The rationale behind the gold standard is simple: the value of any countries' currency is fixed to a tangible commodity, and thus there is almost no problem with the inflation of currency. In Europe, there were several countries that got off the gold standard in the early 1930's. The major change to current economic policy was when Great Britain, who had been on-again off-again with the gold standard, finally stayed off the gold standard for good. John Maynard Keynes, the chief architect of government expenditures seen during the great depression, suggested that the Bank of England should be the entity charged with printing currency. In doing this, he also warned of the perils of inflation. Keynes said: "By a continuous process of inflation, governments can confiscate, secretly and unobserved, an important part of the wealth of their citizens. By this method, they not only confiscate, but they confiscate arbitrarily; and while the process impoverishes many, it actually enriches some."

In order to prevent future collapses that were seen during the great depression, the Bretton Woods agreement in 1944 enacted the International Monetary Fund. The IMF created a mechanism where various world currencies could be converted to dollars and then the dollars could be converted to gold. So, in essence, most world currencies were indirectly on the gold standard. In turn, the U.S.

promised to fix the price of gold at $35 an ounce.

The problem that governments had with the gold standard is that they must balance their budgets or have the capacity to borrow money. So, it would be very difficult to finance massive government expenditures like the New Deal or Lyndon Johnson's Great Society. When Johnson enacted the Great Society acts such as Medicare and Medicaid, the U.S. was forced into severe deficit spending. At the time, the U.S. began to print significantly more money than had been printed early in the century. These heavy levels of printing money set the stage for the double digit inflation seen throughout the 1970's.

Keynes had specifically warned that if we did not have a gold standard, then the central banks would have to be prudent in the printing of money. Because of mounting pressure to pay for the Great Society and France purchasing gold in order to free itself from the U.S. dollar, Nixon officially took the U.S. off the gold standard in 1971. At the time, the U.S. dollar was still the standard for the world. We convinced the world that with our sound economic policy, there was no reason to fear the dollar's collapse.

The Track Record of Keynesian Economics
Keynesian Economics in rooted in the principle that in times of recession or depression, the government must increase its expenditures to match the decrease in private sector expenditures. It is totally irrelevant how the government spends the money. As Keynes puts it, the government should "hire people to dig a hole and fill it up again."

To date, the largest test of Keynesian Economics has been the New Deal. If Keynes was right, the New Deal should have been enough of a stimulus to pull the economy out of the depression. Clearly, it did not even come close. In 1940, after seven full years of New Deal Policies, it was apparent that the New Deal was an unquestioned failure. Two out of three Americans even felt that the New Deal had prolonged the Great Depression. Roosevelt's own Treasury Secretary was despondent over the huge debt levels and lack of economic progress. You would think that this colossal failure of an economic theory would forever end its relevance in economic thought. However, what common sense fails to realize is that free spending politicians are always looking for an excuse…..i.e., an economic theory, to recklessly and needlessly spend money. This is done under the guise of stimulus packages, New Deals, Great Societies, and Wars.

The Justification for Keynes in New Deal
Despite seven full years of abject failure, Keynesians held onto the belief that the New Deal did not go far enough. So you might ask "what would?" The answer by Keynesians is World War II. During World War II, the government took on mass debt and expenditures in order to

fund the war efforts. This, Keynesians argued, was the stimulus the economy needed to get out of the Great Depression. If this doesn't make full sense to you, then consider the following parable.

In the early 1990's, the rapper Hammer achieved worldwide fame and stardom with several huge hits. During this time he financially prospered, making over $30 million. However, his new found prosperity was matched only by his propensity to spend money…and boy did he spend……on his "posse", gold, houses, cars, and many of the other excesses that come along with stardom. Clearly, he thought success would last for an indefinite period of time. It did not. Just a few short years after his rise to fame, he was bankrupt.

Now you may think to yourself the answer is clear as to what happened to Hammer. However, consider this possibility…..that he did not spend enough. If he spent more, good things would have happened.

If there was one more person in his "posse", then that job would create many more. If he had purchased a few more cars then the car dealers would have stayed in business longer and employed more people. Basically, if he had spent more money then the economy would have been better and people would have had more money to buy his records. And thus, his career and fortunes would have been infinitely improved. This is the Keynesian theory of Hammer, the story of a financial empire gone awry.

Other Keynesian Trials
There have been other notable failures of Keynesian Economic Theory. Lyndon Johnson, much like Herbert Hoover, sought to eradicate poverty in the U.S. However, much like Hoover 3 decades before him, he failed miserably. The Great Society brought about such well known social programs such as Medicare and Medicaid. However, the economy in the 1960's at the start of the Great Society was robust, with low unemployment and

steady job growth. This came to a rapid end with the mass increase in government expenditures. In addition, this set the course for the stagflation, a combination of recession and high inflation, seen throughout the 1970's.

Until it happened in the U.S. in the 1970's, Keynesians believed that stagflation was not possible. The belief is that high unemployment is associated with high interest rates. If employment is high, then there will be greater demand which raises prices. So, it would be theoretically implausible to have both stagnant economic growth and inflation. Once again, the Keynesians were wrong. Not only did we have stagflation but we had it for the better part of a decade. Further, Keynesian policies once again failed to get us out of stagflation. It was Paul Volker, Chairman of the Federal Reserve under Ronald Reagan, who finally got us out of the stagflation cycle by dramatically decreasing the money supply and plunging us into a deep recession in 1979. Thus, the Federal Reserve treatment for the problem of inflation or stagflation is decreasing the money supply, thereby raising interest rates.

Despite the widespread failures of Keynesian economic policy, there is still a widespread belief that the use of Keynesian polices is the answer to get us out of the current financial mess we are in. I could not disagree more. Between the New Deal and the Great Society, we have almost two decades of data showing that Keynesian Economics is not going to work. The Next Great Depression is not going to be caused by Wall Street greed or by the sub-prime mortgage meltdown, but rather by the over the top Keynesian response of the government.

In the early part of 2009 alone, the government has committed itself to printing $2.6 trillion, which is more than we have printed since the founding of our nation. The belief is that the deflationary pressures of a deep recession will offset the inflationary pressures of printing money. If they are wrong, then the Federal Reserve has put itself in a box it cannot get out of. If they raise interest rates and cut the money supply as Volker did, they risk destroying banks that will take years to recover from the current crisis. If they let it go, we have inflation unlike anything we have ever seen, causing a collapse of the U.S. dollar. Either way, we're screwed.

Chapter 8
The Coming Storm

When asked how something like this can happen, my most common response is "how much time do you have?" When I say this, I am very serious. There are so many factors at play, from very poor legislation and government oversight to banks just making very stupid loans. What may be even more important than how we got here is the solutions that are currently being implemented. In my opinion, the Next Great Depression will the result of he policies that are currently being implemented rather than the financial collapse we are now in.

To understand the context of what has happened, you must first understand how the individuals involved in the crisis view it, especially Ben Bernake. Chairman Bernake wrote his doctoral dissertation and many articles on the Great Depression. His view is that the Great Depression was a result of the Federal Reserve keeping interest rates too low in the 1920's and then raising rates too fast. After the stock market crash of 1929, the

Federal Reserve did not loosen its monetary policy largely because of the heavy criticism it received for keeping the money supply loose for so long. So, when the market crashed, they did exactly the opposite. Bernake is a monetarist, which means that he believes that if the Federal Reserve had given adequate liquidity to the markets after the stock market crash and before the banks collapsed in 1933, the Great Depression would have been another ordinary recession. This belief explains his meeting with Congressional members in which advised that if we didn't move forward with a $700 billion bailout of banks, that we would have another Great Depression. Bernake really believes that the government should print money and spend its way out of the situation. He even said in a speech years ago that the treasury should have fired up the printing presses and printed large amounts of money in response to the deflation seen in the 1930's. As a matter of fact, that is exactly what we're doing right now. The problem is that this is only a theory of monetarists. There is no way we can take the hypothesis to a lab and test it before trying it on humans. For the sake of all of us, I hope he is right...but I'm afraid he is not.

There is a significant difference between now and the Great Depression that Chairman Bernake fails to acknowledge. During the 1930's, the U.S. did not have a national debt of $11 trillion. When we talk about $700 billion bailouts, the question is where exactly the money comes from. For decades, the government has generally spent more than it brings in and does not pay off the national debt. When debt becomes due, more debt is issued to pay for the old debt. Most of our national debt is owed to China and India. To pay these countries, we must issue more debt.

There was a significant problem after the bailout and the stimulus package were announced. For the first time, the U.S. could not sell all the debt it wanted to.

So, to fund the bailout, the U.S. simply printed the money. This devalued the currency, so the purchasing power of every dollar decreased. Think about this when you travel to Europe and the dollar buys relatively little or when Havana cab drivers will only accept Euros and not dollars. The more money we print, the more the dollar is devalued.

To date, most estimates have the U.S. government printing upwards of $2 trillion dollars. To give you an idea of exactly how much $2 trillion dollars is, consider the following it would buy:
1. Every citizen of Los Angeles a new Ferrari......twice
2. A Rolex watch for every man in the U.S.
3. Two Tiffany's starfish diamond pendants for every woman in the U.S.
4. Four 73' high definition televisions for every home in the U.S.

5. It is more than twice than the GDP of Saudi Arabia
6. It is approximately 2.5 years worth of all federal income taxes collected in the U.S.

You need not look to far back in history to find a rapid devaluation of a major currency. In 1998, the Russian Ruble was rapidly devalued. At the time, Russia could not pay the bonds it had previously issued. So, they went to the printing press and simply printed money. Also, Zimbabwe has had a notorious recent history of printing money. They now have a billion dollar bill. A U.S. treasury official was recently asked how what the U.S. is doing is different from Zimbabwe. He could not give an answer other than to sidestep the question.

Thus far, my prediction about what would transpire has been very accurate. I hope this does not continue for the sake of our country. However, this is my opinion of what's to come. There are two possible scenarios--neither of which has a happy ending.

1. The actions taken by the Federal Reserve along with the bailout unfreeze the credit markets to the point where loans can be made again. Soon, the problem will not be the availability of credit but the rapid devaluation of the dollar. When prices rapidly inflate after the currency hits the market, what will the Federal Reserve do then? If they contract the money supply, do banks survive? If they leave interest rates low, will another bubble be created? We've already had a real estate bubble and a stock market bubble. Is our currency the next bubble to burst? The other problem is when will we get to the point of no return in regards to paying down our national debt? There will be no way we can issue new debt because the market is saturated. The main problem is that the only way the

existing debt can be paid is by going to the printing press once again and printing more money. At that point, does the dollar become the ruble in 1998? This is the scenario I think is most likely.

2. The second scenario is a grim one and involves every problem listed in scenario 1. In this scenario, the treasury throws $700 billion at the banks and another $1.3 trillion in a stimulus and still credit markets do not unfreeze. When does Congress put and end to the bailouts if they don't work? When Hank Paulson was asked what would happen if Congress did not pass the bailout, his response was "heaven help us." What happens if the whole plan doesn't work? Then all of scenario 1 would happen with no positive externality. In this scenario, we are in something far worse than the Great Depression.

In my opinion, the bailout was a huge mistake. This is what I think should have been done...and still should be done:

1. Raise FDIC insurance to $5 million from $250,000. The reason that Indy Mac, WAMU, and others collapsed was a modern day run on the banks, when depositors with large amounts of money withdrew it because of the uneasiness of having such a small amount insured. This would have prevented, and still would prevent, many bank failures.
2. Our income tax system should be thrown out the window and replaced with the Fair Tax, which is a 23 cent national sales tax that would replace income tax, FICA, and Medicare taxes. This would accomplish something the bailout never could. First, over $8 trillion in U.S. dollars is held in bank accounts in the Cayman Islands and in Luxembourg, which are havens for hiding money for the purposes of

avoiding income tax. Imagine what kind of "stimulus" we could have if any portion of $8 trillion was infused into our economy and banking system! Second, the IRS is a cash drain to the taxpayers. The budget for the IRS is more money than we spend in Iraq! This would eliminate a huge government expense while encouraging businesses and money to come back to the U.S. There is no one single thing that could help our economy more than the Fair Tax.

3. Sarbanes-Oxley should be repealed. It has chased away businesses and cost an exorbitant amount in compliance costs. Further, the concept of "mark-to market" accounting has crippled banks in their ability to lend.

In conclusion, although the roots of what happened started in 1998, it is my belief that it was actually 9/11 which best typifies what happened in this financial crisis. The attacks of 9/11 were a direct attack on the U.S. financial system. It was deliberately meant to cripple our economy, but it failed. Our people proved resilient and our economy recovered. The sad truth is that Al Qaeda could not do to our economy we ultimately did to ourselves.

CPSIA information can be obtained at www.ICGtesting.com
Printed in the USA
BVOW041837210812

298474BV00005B/8/P